Living with
Joy

Living with
Joy

Donald McKinney

ABINGDON / Nashville

LIVING WITH JOY

Copyright © 1976 by Abingdon

Library of Congress Cataloging in Publication Data

McKinney, Donald, 1909-
    Living with joy.
    1. Meditations. I. Title.
BV4832.2.M1994   242′.4   76-8203

ISBN 0-687-22375-X

MANUFACTURED BY THE PARTHENON PRESS AT
NASHVILLE, TENNESSEE, UNITED STATES OF AMERICA

To Elaine Rohe,
one of God's chosen people

Preface

Every life has both dark and cheerful hours. You are fortunate if you have learned that happiness in life comes in choosing which to remember.

This book is about some of the cheerful hours that have touched lives. Memory is a benediction when you are alone. The people you have met and loved throughout the years are a reflection in your life today.

But the past is only one dimension of your life. There is a motto on my library door that I read every morning: Today Is the First Day of the Rest of Your Life. There is a past, but there is also a present. Happiness can be real in your life each morning if you say, "What new friend will I meet today?"

The inspiration for this book came one Sunday morning when I spoke to the men and women who live at Interfaith Apartments, Richmond, Indiana. I used Luke 2:10 as my text, "I bring you good tidings of great joy." What I said to them is true about you. Back of every life are a home, children, vocations that enriched the communities in which you have lived. When God touches the human heart, man is not content to just work at a job. Many of you find a deep satisfaction and richness in life by doing volunteer work in hospitals, day nurseries, or church, writing cards and letters, sharing the mellowness and beauty of your life with others.

Living With Joy

A senior student in psychology wrote in a teacher's yearbook in 1967, "You are one of the few teachers and adults who really understand us and our problems. This has been the first class I have ever taken where students have really been able to express their opinions." The words of this seventeen-year-old student are a tribute to the boys and girls who stimulated a classroom situation for learning and sharing problems, hopes, and dreams.

These people are all around you, and you are a happy person if you can listen to others who need to talk. You can feel deep within you the touch of God's hand—yes, you are doing what you can to "feed Christ's sheep."

Each day we build upon the past. The past means people. It is to these people who have smiled and touched and loved that this book is written.

Each story is, I hope, a challenge to you to lift your eyes to the truth spoken in the Holy Bible that the best is yet to be, that there are still greater things for you to do. As long as you cherish faith in yourself and in God, as long as you face each new day with a positive attitude and joy in your heart, you will always be young.

DONALD McKINNEY

Contents

For These Hands

I have set the Lord always before me; because he is at my right hand.   *—Psalm 16:8*

Thank you, God, for these hands. May they ever be used in your service.

Sometimes we accept without thinking the common things of life, like our hands. We look at the sunset and marvel. We stand breathless at the sight of the shimmering wings of a Cecropia moth against the window screen. The smell of browning chicken in a big skillet, the newly polished automobile, the marvel of color television are all so real. But who ever looks at hands?

How long has it been since you last sat in a chair and held the palms of your hands before you? Gently fold your fingers and straighten them out again. How wonderful!

I remember when you brought your doll to me. She had a broken arm, and tears should not have been in the eyes of one so young. When my hands made the arm as good as new you smiled and gave me a hug and a kiss on the cheek.

I remember when you were afraid of the violent storm, and you ran into my sheltering arms, and my hands stroked your head, and I told you not to be afraid.

These hands have carried heavy sacks of groceries, have hemmed your dress for graduation, have removed a tiny splinter from a child's foot. These hands lifted you tenderly upon the operating table. These hands per-

11

formed a delicate cataract operation that gave you back your sight. They have written words of joy and love on the card that went to you when you were ill.

Just two hands, God. Thank you. These hands tied the blue bow on your birthday present, touched the hands of so many in greeting at church, waved to friends who stood on the deck of an ocean liner.

These hands raked the leaves, made the beds, played the organ at the wedding, helped you take your first steps. They opened the box of dog biscuits and fed your puppy when you were away for the night.

Just two hands. How did you know to make them so wonderful, God? How did you know I needed two hands? How could you be so wise? I could not button my shirt with one hand or tie my shoes or wash dishes or nail a board on a fence.

I think, as I sit here, of all that these hands have done for me through the years. I think of what they can still do. They held the towel today to dry my grandson after his bath. They held the book I read. They picked up the Easter card you sent that I might read your words the tenth time.

How beautiful are the lines in the hands, the shape, the texture, the softness. My fingers bend and unbend when I tell them to. But when I shell beans or type, I give them no orders. My fingers and hands know what to do. Have I told you lately, God, thank you for these hands.

Thanks for the Memory

This is my commandment, That ye love one another, as I have loved you.   *—John 15:12*

Sometimes you do have a choice of being the kind of person you want to be. Not once, but many times in life, you may come to a fork in the road—one road leading to regret and sorrow and the other to joy and happiness. If you love others, the road you take will help them to climb.

Robert Manning tells the story of a lonely, motherless boy of fourteen years who met two new teachers in his freshman year of high school. One said to him, "I don't like your attitude." The other said, "I think you are a very fine boy." Because he wanted to be happy, the boy chose to remember the teacher who understood the dream in his heart. The last day of school he walked into her room, bashful, half-afraid, and stammered out the words, "I want to thank you for what you said to me one day last October. I have never forgotten your words."

Her picture was on his desk throughout his college years, and she was to influence his life and life's work for half a century. Then, on her fiftieth college anniversary at Earlham College they met for the first time since high school days.

"I wouldn't have known you," Robert Manning said. "You have changed so much in fifty years." And before the seventy-two-year-old teacher could reply, Robert Manning added, "I had forgotten how beautiful you *are.*"

13

Yes, she had the thinning gray hair and wrinkles that seventy-two years bring, but the glow of joy and love was eternal in her eyes and smile. The teacher who said, "I don't like your attitude," was there too. What a contrast! Somewhere along the way she had lost the glow of life.

If you are a positive thinker, if you look for the good in others, if you fill your heart with joy, it is written in your face for all to see. If you are not this kind of person you *can* be. Today is the first day of the rest of your life.

Many of the great Bible stories are about human relationships. Jesus Christ reached out and lifted men and women into a new life. He said again and again, "Go . . . from this day you are free . . . your faith hath made you whole . . . neither do I condemn you . . . come and follow me . . . you can live again."

Young people, as well as old, make mistakes many times. Frequently the sense of guilt weighs heavily upon the mind. Look up today and live. This is why Jesus Christ came into the world that man might have life. There are people, and you may be one of them, who have touched this magic power within and every day find opportunity to love others. Your name may never appear upon a stained-glass window in a church, but it will be enshrined forever in the hearts of those you have cared for.

One teacher is remembered because she caused a boy to lift his eyes and to see himself as a person. Somewhere someone is saying about you, "Thanks for the memory."

14

This Is My
Father's World

*In the beginning God created the heaven and the earth.
. . . and God saw that it was good.*   *—Genesis 1:1, 21*

Last night while you slept, white flakes of snow fell
silently to the ground. No two of the symmetrical forms
were alike. When you awakened, the tree limbs were
bent with the lacy mantle of white.

You stand with your nose pressed against the window
pane. It seems only yesterday that the fence rows and
the woods were aflame with the autumn colors, colors of
red and yellow and scarlet and brown.

There is no life in the branches of the trees. The
fledglings have long since gone. How do the birds know
to fly to a warm climate? How can they fly for a thousand miles and know where to go? How can a bird fly at
all?

It was only yesterday that you turned the soil in your
garden, dropped brown seeds in furrows, covered tu-
bers and bulbs. Only yesterday that you carried a bounti-
ful crop into the house and stocked your basement with
canned peaches, green beans, tomatoes, and jelly and
pumpkins and apples.

My Father's world! How certain you are that he is
never-changing in his management of the world. The
tiny, nondescript bulb you cover with soil will burst into
a red tulip, the paperlike seed into a zinnia. The white
blossoms of the apple tree turn into fruit to fill your
baskets in the basement. And there will be corn and hay

to store in your barn, and this will be the means of bringing butter and milk to your table. What a miracle for a cow to make milk out of hay and corn!

You were cozy all night while you slept through the snow's falling on your roof and the ground. The blankets gave you no heat. They only kept the heat from your body near to you so that you warmed yourself. While you were sleeping the tiredness of your legs and arms went away someplace. You turn away from your window, turn a knob on the wall, and heat begins to come into your room. Do your miracles ever cease, God? I struck a match last night and lighted a candle. I said, "Where did the light come from?" I blew out the candle and I said, "Where did the light go?"

You hear your sister singing as she comes up the stairs, and all of a sudden a bundle of fur flies through the air and almost upsets you—your dog. He has waited hours to be with you. The faith and loyalty of a dog. Who made it so?

It is not just another day. Suddenly it is a special day, a new day. A day of wonderment. There is a twinkle in your father's eye as he describes the antics of a new calf turned out into the snow for the first time, lifting its feet high as if to say, "What is this stuff?"

Funny noises come from a bushel basket on the hot-air register. You lift the burlap-sack covering, and your father explains, "The old sow had them this morning—a fine time to have pigs."

My Father's world! Yesterday the pigs were safe and warm inside their mother, and now this—the miracle of birth.

Mother, I Am
in the Play

And whosoever shall compel thee to go a mile, go with him twain.   *—Matthew 5:41*

My name is Iva Williams. I am a teacher in the Centerdale School in Illinois. The high school play was last night. I am thinking of the night more than a month ago when an angry father came to my home. He was rude to me because he felt justified in being so.

"You promised the class that everyone could be in the junior-class play. What kind of person are you? You know that my daughter with her polio braces can scarcely drag herself across the schoolroom. I think you are mean to raise her hopes. She'd give her life to be in that play. Why weren't you big enough to tell her there was no part for a cripple?"

"No part for a cripple?" I repeated those words after he had gone. There would be a part for a cripple. He hadn't given me a chance to explain. I would tell her the next day. I turned and went back to my desk and the play book. I had given up going out to eat with friends for a week. I had almost finished—just two more nights.

Yes, the play was last night. June Collins, the polio victim, received a standing ovation when the curtain went back up at the end of the play, and she came out on the stage. Mr. Collins and his wife hunted me up backstage, and I looked into the eyes of a man full of tears as he grasped my hand. I know now how he loved and sheltered his daughter.

17

I spent many nights writing a part for June Collins and fitting it into the three-act play. Her role was that of a grandmother. She wore long skirts so that the leg braces did not show. She carried a cane and acted out the role of a sweet and loving old woman.

June Collins made a speech at the party following the play. I felt so small and torn up inside as she thanked me before her classmates for making her dream a reality. The nights I spent writing and rewriting became hours of joy as I listened to her words.

Sometimes teachers are held in low respect by some people. In every age, in every town, in every school, there are teachers to be found in the classroom, like Iva Williams. Teachers who are dedicated to education, to your children. These teachers walk the second mile again and again. We ought to love and support these men and women who give so much and yet are second-class citizens in the eyes of many people.

There have always been more teachers who love and work to help our children succeed than we sometimes realize. How long has it been since you last sent a note to school with your child that said "Thanks"? How long has it been since you walked up to your child's teacher on graduation night and said, "Thanks for helping my child through school"? Teachers are in need of love and appreciation like the rest of us.

God Opens Windows

If any man will come after me, let him deny himself, and take up his cross, and follow me. —Matthew 16:24

What do you do when God says no?

A number of years ago the personnel director of a large New York department store called an employee into his office. She was a woman loved and respected and a lifter of the morale of other workers in the organization. The personnel man wanted to know how she did it. Her story was briefly told.

"When I was a bride of six months my husband was killed in a hunting accident. Three months later I was crossing Broadway with my mother and father when both were struck by an automobile and killed. I blamed myself for not watching them more closely. I was in a sanatorium for weeks trying to fight my way back to reality. One evening in my despair I emptied a box of sleeping pills in the palm of my hand. I had taken them from a nurse's cart.

"A voice spoke to me, but when I looked around I was alone. The voice kept repeating, 'People need you. People need you.' No one needed me. I had no children, no brothers or sisters. Then I realized that it was the voice of God speaking to me. I know it sounds crazy, but my hand opened and the sleeping pills rolled out on my bed. A great peace came over me, and I slept and slept. God spoke to me in the days that followed. If I were to live again I must lose my life for the sake of others. I had to take up my cross and follow him."

When you say to someone, "I know how you feel," you do only if you have had such an experience. One of the rewards of suffering is that it helps you to help others. No person lives alone. Persons are all around you who need your advice, your encouragement, your guidance. It is not surprising that the woman who talked to the personnel manager won the respect and love of others. She cared about them, and she had been close enough to death to know the rich meaning of life.

The *Messiah* was produced by a man who slept in a cold attic and almost starved before giving to the world the great "Hallelujah Chorus" that has thrilled generations.

A young boy was sent home by his teacher with a note stating that he was too dull to learn. He never went back to school. His mother became his teacher, and he became one of the greatest inventors in history. Edison performed thousands of experiments before he triumphantly gave the light bulb to the world.

A girl cried when she ran to her Christmas tree one morning. Instead of toys she found gloves, sweaters, skirts. To give up childhood is not easy. It is not easy to close a door on a past filled with happiness. But God has promised, if you trust him, to open other doors.

Reach out and take his hand and follow him. Take others with you into a life of hope and faith and joy.

I Remember You

I met you for the first time when I was in the second grade and your father brought you to the door of our one-room brick school. You were our new music teacher. You played the organ and gave us the first music books we had ever seen, except for the church hymnal. You taught us to read notes. You lifted us on a magic carpet and took us to halls of princes and kings and faraway places.

In winter your father sometimes brought you in a sleigh. I remember the big fox muff that kept your hands warm so that you could play and the big blue knitted scarf you wrapped around your neck.

You were so beautiful. You always smelled so good. You wore golden earrings and always had a gold necklace and jeweled rings. You patted us on the arm and praised us for being brave enough to open our mouths and make sounds. You were from what seemed to be another world. We were farm children who had never traveled more than a few miles from home. We all knew the mud and drudgery of the farm. We looked forward to your coming; it was like a birthday, like Christmas, like a vacation.

How you must have loved us. You took the runny-nosed children, the poorly dressed, the lonely and gave them a dream. Sometimes you opened a new world for a

21

child who could not remember his multiplication tables and history dates. He found he had a voice and could sing. For the first time he felt successful, standing before the packed schoolroom and singing at a Christmas or Easter program. He hummed and whistled the songs you taught him as he milked the cows and walked down the long rows of corn with a hoe in his hand.

When you were a girl your father took you every Saturday morning to the little station at Olive Hill where you caught a train to Richmond to take your violin lesson. You became a teacher and helped others to have roses in life.

That was more than fifty years ago. And then one evening I read that you were living in my town, had moved back after your husband's death, a man whose magnificent career as a teacher and school administrator you had shared. I went to see you. People change in fifty-one years; you had grown more beautiful, more mellow, more in love with life. It was good to pick up a thread of yesterday.

Every person can bring music into the lives of others. I was impressed deeply at the close of a church service recently when the minister said, "I want every person here this morning to join hands with the person sitting next and say quietly, 'I love you.'"

No three words have a more musical sound. Thank you for helping others to find the music God put into the heart. The days of the one-room school are far away, but memory lives forever.

Gifts Remind Me
of You

My sheep hear my voice, and I know them, and they follow me: And I give unto them eternal life; and they shall never perish. —*John 10:27-28*

Perhaps you have heard someone say or you have read that the gift of oneself is the greatest gift of all. Some of the most treasured possessions you have in your home are gifts. Sometimes gifts represent hours of shopping, looking for that something special for someone special—you!

I picked up a card from the bookshelf of a friend not long ago. It was not a birthday card, not an anniversary card, just something beautiful, the picture of a young girl holding a large seashell to her ear and the words, "I am listening to memories of you."

On the desk of my friend was a funny little man with green bushy hair. His hands were spread wide and high and written on his jacket were the words, "We love you this much."

My neighbor to the north of me has a framed letter on his desk which reads, "Upon reflection of the past weeks of teaching, I have experienced feelings of fear, apprehension, fatigue, and aloneness; however, as communications with you evolved, these inward feelings were changed to days of stability, joy, and hope as an emerging teacher.

"You have continuously reassured me that life is an exciting challenge; you have motivated me to search within myself to project an image of genuineness; you

23

have reinforced my conceptions that students are individuals and are in need of kindness, love, and care just as we are. For this I thank you.

"Thus, there are those special few individuals one meets in life—significant others. I'm sure that at this stage in my life's career *you* are my significant other. I will continuously strive to be happy, smiling, and a lover of life as your image so reflects."

The letter is signed DiAnne T. Moore, student teacher in psychology from Indiana University.

Bill Adams mows my grass. He moved down the road about a year ago. I didn't know he was a retired teacher until I stopped in to pay him a few days ago. While his wife went to get him I thumbed through an old yearbook on his desk. I read, "I shall never forget the fun and laughs we had in your class." Another, "Thanks for making me feel welcome at W.H.S." Still another, "In my twelve years of school I have never had a teacher who made me feel that I was an individual and important as much as you have." In small printing, "From that first day of school I have never seen a frown on your face. You are a real great guy." I never dreamed that Bill's life went beyond mowing my grass.

You have enriched the lives of others by giving yourself. To encourage, to share, to say "You are not alone," is the giving of yourself. Thank you for the gift of yourself.

Man Cannot Live
Without Love

Though I have the gift of prophecy . . . and all knowledge; and though I have all faith . . . and have not charity, I am nothing. —*I Corinthians 13:2*

When you were a child you were taught that a person must have food, clothing, and shelter to live. Man's most essential need for life was omitted—the need to be loved.

A person may be richly dressed to be protected from heat and cold. A person may feast at a banquet table or live in an electrically heated house. But if he does not have love he is nothing, so says the writer of Corinthians.

All living things flourish with love. A framed motto in a bookstore reads, A Flower Cannot Live Without Sunshine, A Man Cannot Live Without Love. All plants, from the small blade of grass to the great oak, grow up toward the sun that gives life.

A child unloved the first year of its life has little chance of becoming a warm, loving individual in later life. From the moment a mother holds her child to her breast, that child understands the security of touch.

One Friday afternoon in the year of 1947 I was walking down a side street in Philadelphia. Three small children were sitting on the sidewalk curb with their feet in the gutter. All of them were crying. I asked the oldest girl why they were crying, and she gave me an immediate answer, "We are crying because Billy has a tummy ache."

Truth is simple to a child. The two children who cried

25

with Billy were saying in the best way they knew how, "We understand how you feel, and we are sorry."

A note came to Mrs. Reed. It read, "I know that I would not have lived through the night if you had not come to the hospital and held my hand through the long hours. The touch of your hand and the love that brought you to my bedside gave me the strength to pull through. I heard your prayers in my heart."

How dear are the memories when God leads you to the right place when you are needed. Sixteen-year-old Janice excitedly said at the dinner table, "A new girl came to our school today. She sat in front of me. I asked her to go to lunch with me and to play with me at noon. You should have seen her eyes light up."

"Yes, Janice, she left all her friends at the school she came from. You made her feel she was wanted. She will be your friend for life. I'm glad you helped her."

A widow of seventy-six held my hand for five minutes last Sunday. I spoke at a retirement home where she lives. She said, "You come because you love us." How lonely the room that has become her home must sometimes be. There are times when she dreams of the "big house," her husband, her children. "Please come back and see us" is an invitation we should never refuse.

Give someone a chance to hold your hand. Give one hour, one afternoon a week if you can, to visit retirement and nursing homes. Share your love with the people who work across the desk from you. They all need you.

In Remembrance

Silver and gold have I none; but such as I have give I thee.   *—Acts 3:6*

Forty-two years ago you gave a graduating college man a book of inspirational poems. You wrote in the inside cover, "In Remembrance." Then you boarded your train for a faraway city.

Have you ever wondered about your gift? Was it carelessly read and hidden on a top shelf to gather dust? Was it ever read?

If you come back you will find the book on my desk, but you will not recognize it. The green cloth cover is faded and falling apart. The pages are marked and tattered. The first poem has been read endless times to young people, in church, in school, in the hospital to the ill, in the nursing home. It is called "The Starlit Hill" by Ralph Spaulding Cushman. (*Hilltop Verses and Prayers* [Nashville: Abingdon-Cokesbury Press, 1945] p. 15).

> There was a night,
> There was a hill,
>   There was a starlit sky;
> An upturned face
> That hardly sensed
>   The night wind blowing by.
>
> There was a Voice—
> No human voice—
>   I heard it clear and still;
> And since that night,

27

And since that Voice,
I've loved each starlit hill.

You did not know that when you gave this book you were giving a part of yourself, that your gift would have the effect of a stone dropped in a pool of water, sending out waves in all directions. You have been a means of helping others to share in the beautiful and enduring faith of Cushman.

You put quotation marks around *In Remembrance*. You might have written the words just moments ago. The words are a part of you. Each time I pick up the book I think of the joy and beauty that you have brought into the lives of so many people. You inspired all of us who knew you; you gave us courage; you gave us a sense of mission in life. You and I may meet again upon some busy street, at a college reunion, and talk about the old days.

You have so much to give. The small gift is sometimes the most cherished gift. Anyone could have dropped a coin in the hand of the man at the gate. But when Peter spoke to this man he demanded that he do something for himself, that he get up and walk; and he did because someone had faith in him. You can instill faith in others. To simply say "God loves you" can be music in the ears of one who struggles to rise.

It was just a small book given in remembrance, but it was a gift of love, and that is a priceless gift.

An Apple Tree in Bloom

And God said, Let the earth bring forth . . . the fruit
tree yielding fruit . . . and it was so.   *—Genesis 1:11*

Man is like an apple tree in many ways. He sprouts,
blossoms, matures, bears fruit. But man is more. He has
a soul. He has the power to dream, to grow in the spirit,
to walk the second mile with his neighbor.

Many years ago I stepped upon English soil for the
first time to go to college. Within hours I found myself
having tea on the lush grounds of the university, talking
to students from France, Jamaica, Sweden, Norway, Hol-
land, New Zealand, Lebanon, Denmark, Hong Kong,
China, Switzerland, Scotland, Germany, British Guiana,
and England.

We spoke the same language. We were filled with
courage and hope for a better world. We all believed
deeply and wanted to be a part of God's working plan
in bringing in this new world. We were alike in having
a deep abiding love for all mankind.

There was a difference. Some of these students had
come from battle-scarred towns and cities in Europe.
Many had lost close relatives in the war which had just
ended. Three came from concentration camps where
man's inhumanity to man had reached new depths in a
civilized world.

England is a fairyland of houses, gardens of roses,
foxgloves, tulips, rhododendrons. Quaint little shops delight the newcomer. Until recently the slow-moving tram

stopped in the middle of the block when tea time came, and even now machines shut down in factories when tea kettles are put on hot plates for this English custom.

England is old, but there is always a new crop of red-cheeked children spilling out into the streets and the playing fields. There is endless discussion of politics and economics in the social clubs for the millions—the pubs.

But what I remember most was the apple tree that grew just outside my dormitory window. During my first week of school in April it was a greening apple tree with swelling red-tipped buds. Next it was covered with a mantle of white, followed by small apples.

There was other life in the tree too, the beginning of a robin's nest. From the four blue eggs hatched fledglings that seemed to be all mouths gaping up. Feathers appeared and the fledglings stood on the edge of the nest and ventured in faltering flight to a small limb. Then the nest was empty. And the tree—in time the leaves fluttered to the ground and the limbs were bare. The apples had been picked.

Man is like an apple tree. The summer students came to plant a seed of hope for a weary world. The dormitory and the classroom became alive with discussions, ways to build this better world.

I walked out of an empty dormitory to catch my plane for home. The leaves were drifting across the lawn. Like the apples that had been shipped to faraway places, the students had departed. But I knew the college rooms would be filled again, there would be another spring, and I must hurry on my mission to speak for a new dawn of brotherhood.

"How Great Thou Art"

She has done a beautiful thing to me . . . . Wherever this gospel is preached in the whole world, what she has done will be told in memory of her.

—*Matthew 26:10-13 RSV*

I remember Sue. She stood beside the church pulpit one Sunday morning. The reds and purples from the stained-glass window made a halo around her head as the sun's rays reached across the interior of the church. Our hearts were lifted as the organ music and the words of "How Great Thou Art" dimmed the cares and problems of our lives.

You were so beautiful, Sue. Did you know the joy and peace you brought into our hearts? You touched us as the angel chorus touched the hearts of the shepherds on the night that Jesus was born. Your voice was a candle leading us up the valley to the mountaintop where we might hope again. And when the words of your song ended we closed our eyes and felt the benediction of your words.

I watched your fingers, Carol, as they touched the keys of the organ until the last notes of "How Great Thou Art" died away. You sat tall, and the look in your eyes helped us to feel the presence of God. What a miracle that fingers can move and create such heavenly music!

God stands before us every day. He does not ask us to sing or play an organ. Sometimes he just asks that we smile to a lonely person or that we reach out and touch someone in sorrow. He comes into our lives again and again that we may be a channel of his love to make the world happier. Thank you, God, for helping us to help others and to know that you care.

When I think of Sue and Carol I think of the dark valleys they have walked through. It is for this reason that the warmth of their love reaches out to us in understanding. Your Son walked the road of darkness too, God. But you lifted him out of the darkness, and he left man on the mountaintop. Thank you for the spirit in our lives that makes us want to share what we can with others.

I shall always remember, Sue and Carol, the delight I saw in the eyes of the people you greeted that morning in church and the moment when you put your arms around me and said good-bye. These things we remember, God, when we sit alone, when we rest our heads upon our pillows at night; our thoughts are of the great men and women who have brought happiness to us.

Somewhere there is a wonderful musical family, mothered by Sue and Carol, bringing song and instrument joys to others.

The church is empty now. There is no one seated at the organ, no halo of red and purple where she stood singing that morning. But if I close my eyes I see her standing there. I see the fingers move across the keys. And I feel so close to you, God. I know that when we share that which is good it goes on and on and on.

Journey into Greatness

Now the Lord said unto Abram, Get thee out of thy country, and from thy kindred . . . unto a land that I will shew thee.   —*Genesis 12:1*

When Norbert Silbiger sat in a World War II concentration camp and pieced together costumes from rags, after being deported from his native Vienna, he did not know that someday he would bring to Richmond, Indiana, civic theater at its best.

Today, in his retirement, the eyes of this brilliant play director reflect a memory of pain and triumph. For a generation he selected people to delight thousands, sitting before the footlights. In comedy, tragedy, and musicals the Richmond civic theater players brought culture to a city that has made the name of Norbert Silbiger a legend.

Because he was an intellectual, a lover of art, a man of deep piety for his fellowmen, Norbert Silbiger was torn from his Vienna home and, grateful that he lived, produced plays in his prison camp to soften the lives of the starving and hopeless inmates surrounding him.

Then, as by a miracle of God's hands, Quakerism reached across the sea to him, and this humble little man came to Quaker Hill, wearing a suit of clothes that had been given to him. His Austria was no more, and he turned his eyes to the nation that had befriended him and asked what he could do.

The answer was become a leader in the establishment of a theater and become its director. For many years there was a long waiting list for tickets. Norbert

Silbiger could have gone to Chicago, New York, Hollywood, but he chose to remain in the midst of the people who had befriended him.

It was a proud day in the lives of the citizens of Richmond when Earlham College in June of 1968 bestowed the honorary degree of doctor of humane letters upon the man who had never sought honor. The degree is evidence that here in the United States a man can still rise to the top, that national origin, race, family name are not a hindrance to achievement.

The memory of Norbert Silbiger, sitting in the fourth row of the theater during rehearsal and saying "You can do it, I know you can" to a stumbling actor, endeared this humble director to all who sang and danced and laughed and talked upon the stage.

Across the front of the theater the name *Norbert Silbiger Theater* is more than a name. He was the theater. It was a golden age when he built the theater into one of the greatest civic theaters in the Midwest.

Norbert Silbiger will never see his native land again. There is a sadness in his eyes as he remembers his childhood. There are tears in his eyes when he thinks of the land that extended its hand and heart to him, the United States of America.

You Were So Young
and So Beautiful

The flowers appear on the earth; the time of the singing of birds is come.   *—Song of Solomon 2:12*

You noticed her for the first time that September morning, the opening day of school. She bumped into you at the door when you came in from the playground, summoned by the teacher ringing the bell.

She was a new girl. She smiled in a shy way and said, "I didn't mean to bump you." She took her seat two desks ahead of you. Her hair was short and curly, almost bald from the illness of scarlet fever. Her face was covered with big brown freckles. The white dress with red dots was stiffly starched. She was the most beautiful girl you had ever seen, and you were deeply in love with her and had been for exactly four minutes.

To be in love! You were in the seventh grade and all of twelve years old. It was not your first love, but this was different. When you were in the fifth grade you were in love with Miss Thomas. Miss Thomas came from the city and was really ignorant about farms and farming. You were always having to explain farming to her. Then one Thanksgiving your father said, "Why, she spent several summers on her grandfather's farm over near Greensfork. She drove a team, fed the pigs, and did about everything for him." Young as I was I understood. She pretended to be uninformed to get us to talk. We really learned how to express ourselves in her class.

When winter came, Miss Thomas brought a kettle and

put it on top of the big heating stove in the schoolroom. She would boil potatoes, heat vegetable soup for our cups, or some other hot food to go with the cold lunch from home.

On nice days she went outside and played rabbit and tag with us. It was always fun to catch her. One day when I caught her she put her arm around me and gave me a hug. I knew then I would marry her when I grew up. She was a mother to many of the children, the only mother some of them had.

And then, after bumping the new girl at the door, I knew I couldn't marry my fifth-grade teacher. As I stared at my new girl two seats ahead I knew that my love for her was a mature love, not a puppy love. This would last forever. "Harold Williams, I've called your name twice. Are you here this morning?" Miss Cloud was looking straight at me. I came to attention.

"You may pass out the chalk, and then I want everyone to go to the blackboard and write his or her name."

As I walked to the front of the room I wanted to poke Harry Bell. He was sitting right across from my girl, and he was talking to her. Then Miss Cloud spoke again.

"And, Harold, when you are through I want you to exchange seats with Harry. The desks will fit better." We all knew Harry was being punished for whispering. I sat across from my new girl, Beth Ann, and when I lent her a pencil my fingers touched hers. I knew she belonged to me forever.

An Old Yearbook

Study to shew thyself approved unto God, a workman that needeth not to be ashamed. —II Timothy 2:15

I opened an old yearbook from Earlham College today and thumbed through the pages of the faculty. They were giants in their day, Arthur M. Charles, Clara Comstock, Charles E. Cosand, Ruby Davis, Anna Eves, Murvel Garner, Elmer Grant, Allen D. Hole, Ella Bond Johnson, Florence Long, Millard S. Markle, Elsie Marshall, Martha Pick, E. Merrill Root, Maurice O. Ross, Edwin P. Trueblood, George Van Dyke, and Ernest Wildman.

You have only to change the names and come up with the scholars who stood at the front of classrooms in colleges all over this nation and encouraged students to think and grow and know. For a few brilliant years the spark of divinity guided our college professors in the directing of young minds to prepare for a world in which they were to live.

With some fears and trembling you got aboard a train or an interurban forty years ago to travel to a faraway town, and there you stepped upon what was to become to you the hallowed ground of a college and university. You left behind the narrow, complacent, provincial community. It was a good place for a child to grow up because it meant security, protection from the world.

You can't go back to the childhood world. You

wouldn't want to go back. The doctor—with his four bottles of colored pills and time to sit by a bedside and wish he had the knowledge to save lives—the horse and buggy, the ax and the woodpile, the brick house with the straw mattresses, were all a part of that yesterday.

You scan the pages of the seniors in the old yearbook. Some contributed greatly to the fields of science and medicine with their discoveries. Others became teachers, writers, artists, musicians. Some became industrialists, farmers, clergymen, clerks, salesmen, mothers.

The old yearbook brings back memories of the date to the college spring dance, the wilted corsage, and the goodnight kiss outside the dormitory, and many are the memories of the long walks across the tree-shaded campus and the plans for after college.

You go back for alumni day. The library is new. The old English Building is gone. There is a new football field. And who are the people walking around in blue jeans and wearing beards? You remember the first night you went to the dining hall in a white shirt and were told, "You can come in this time, but tomorrow evening wear a tie and a coat for dinner."

These kids! You go back for commencement only to find there are no caps and gowns. A rental fee of six thousand dollars was collected from the seniors and the check sent to buy milk and soup for refugee children in the Middle East. How true it is that we live in a changing world.

You Touched My Heart

For I was an hungered, and ye gave me meat: I was thirsty, and ye gave me drink: I was a stranger, and ye took me in . . . I was sick, and ye visited me.
—*Matthew 25:35-36*

I have just returned from Reid Memorial Hospital. My name is Joyce Truesdale, but my name does not matter. There are many like me. I am thinking about you tonight, so many of you, for without your love and your care I would not have lived. Do you understand why I love you?

When the doctor said I had to go for an operation, I was afraid I would never come home. With reluctant hands I packed a handbag with a few personal things. There were tears in my eyes when I closed the front door of my home and got into my neighbor's car to go to the hospital.

Within a few minutes I walked through the doors of the hospital and found myself in a strange new world. I was surrounded by people in white uniforms. I felt myself being eased into a wheelchair. A soft voice said, "Just a few questions and then you will be taken to your room."

Within minutes I was in a white gown and tucked into bed. A nurse touched my shoulder, "I can tell this is your first trip to the hospital. You do not need to be afraid. You have the best doctor in his field."

It seemed only minutes later that I awakened. My mind was not clear. A young woman in white hurried to my bedside, and I whispered to her, "How soon will they operate?"

"You are in the recovery room. Your operation was over two hours ago. You were a perfect patient."

The operation over? I began to piece parts together. Slowly the past came back. I had been bathed, given a sedative just after the surgeon had come to my room to explain the operation. And there was another young man who came in and explained to me how I would sleep and feel no pain. Then I slipped into darkness.

Lonely in a hospital? The day after my operation I became a person again. A woman from the Reid Auxiliary came in wearing a smile, "Is there anything I can get for you?" An aide helped me sit up in bed. She took the top off my orange and opened my milk carton.

I thanked the Candy Striper for the first potted flower carried into my room. My heart warmed to the friendly greeting of the Red Cross volunteer who brought me the morning cards. Each card whispered, "I am thinking of you."

These people who staff our hospitals, those who give of their time freely, do they know, God, what it means to us when they walk the second mile? I pray for them tonight. Bless them, for they touched my heart.

I will always remember that I was a stranger, frightened, until I learned that I was surrounded by people who loved me because I needed them. Someday I want to be one of them. I want to work in a hospital where people are helpless and need me.

When You Are Lonely

A new commandment I give unto you, That ye love one another; as I have loved you. —*John 13:34*

We should be so thankful for the men and women who have chosen to work with the ill, the old, and many times the dying in our nursing homes and hospitals. Sometimes when we are ill we expect so much. But those who care for us seem to understand our frustration in being helpless and having to be waited upon.

Nurses are people. They have children to dress and get off to school, husbands to listen to and go places with. The young women on the staff sometimes cry on their pillows at night over boy problems, and the young men plan for the day when they will have saved enough money to get married.

A shy woman came into my room one morning when I was in the hospital. She was in a yellow uniform, a member of the housekeeping staff. I said to her, "You have been keeping my room so clean. I am always glad when you come in. You have a beautiful smile." She was pleased that I spoke to her. She does not have much education, but she is a person, a vital link in the hospital staff, and I honor her.

Last night I could not sleep. The hospital was quiet. The visitors had gone. A practical nurse came into my room, made my bed, gave me a shoulder massage. She gave me a warm smile, touched my hand, and told me to have a good night's sleep. I slept well. I never saw her again, yet I remember her. She cared for me, a stranger.

A Candy Striper read my cards for me. She lowered my shade. She held a glass of water for me. A nurse carefully dressed my wound from the incision. A doctor filled my room with sunshine.

I closed my eyes and said "thank you" to the women in the kitchen who fixed my tray, to the man who pushed the heavy cart of food to my floor. I said "thank you" to the men who sit behind the desks and study ways to operate a hospital on limited funds and rising costs.

I will never see the young woman, but somewhere hidden away in a laboratory she made the tissue test and her finds were phoned to surgery: "There is no malignancy." He could not do one thing until he heard from her. I thanked the unknown blood donor who gave me life.

Yes, all of these people helped me to live again. I know that back of the starched uniforms are hearts that love and care. Back of the long, stringy hair, the hot-rodding teen-agers, is a kindness I never dreamed of.

Jesus tells of the man who knelt beside the wounded traveler. He tells of the father who rushed to meet a son with a wounded heart. God reminds us that we are the light of the world. I believe. Yes, I believe that what he said is true, for I have been a witness to the unselfish love of those who have said, "Let me help you."

The Old Country School

Children, obey your parents in the Lord: for this is right.
Honour thy father and mother.   *—Ephesians 6:1-2*

It was one of the rare delights of childhood to climb into the buggy with my mother and father and drive to Greensfork in late August. There at the Mosey store my parents bought me farm shoes, overalls, and shirts for the opening of the one-room school. On the way home I held the shoes on my lap with tender possessiveness. The overalls I would wear rolled up at the bottom until they were washed and the legs would shrink and the smell of new cloth would be gone.

When school opened, my willow lunch basket would be packed with fried chicken, apple-jelly sandwiches, gingerbread cake, and a glass of home-canned peaches. While my mother packed my lunch I filled the big wood-box and pumped and carried into the house two buckets of water.

My sister and I walked to school with the Lundy family. We talked about our *city* teacher, plans for Halloween, the two new books in our school library, *Peter Rabbit* and *Mother Westwind's Neighbors*. When it was cold we went immediately into the schoolroom and warmed ourselves around the big jacketed stove until the last bell rang.

Opening exercises might consist of marching around the room to a phonograph record or listening to the teacher read the thrilling adventure of *Cudgel's Cave*.

43

Sometimes we stood at the front of the room and talked about a home experience.

In the fall, on our way home from school, we stopped by the big covered bridge to pick apples from a stray tree. In the fall we hurried home to pick up potatoes until darkness fell and our backs were broken from bending over. We raked the leaves and drove home the cows from the woods pasture.

For breakfast it was almost always fried sausage, baking-powder or soda biscuits, milk and rolled oats. Supper was always a surprise. It might be bread and milk or potato soup and sometimes fried chicken and creamy mashed potatoes with maybe hickory nut cake or homemade ice cream.

Mother often worked in the field beside my father husking corn. She milked the cows, cared for the garden, managed a large flock of chickens, washed with a hand machine, baked the bread, ironed our clothes. My sister and I gathered the eggs, churned the butter, and cleaned lamp chimneys.

Mother was the doctor and bore bravely through the times of mumps, measles, chicken pox, and colds. The only time that I doubted her skill as a doctor was the morning she tied a large bacon rind around my neck and sent me to school. With the fat side to my chest, and sitting next to the school stove, the fat began to melt. It ran down my stomach, my legs, and into my shoes. My teacher removed the bacon rind in the front hall out of sight of my sister who would "tell my mother." I loved that teacher.

Reach for a Star

I will lift up mine eyes unto the hills.   *—Psalm 121:1*

A noted psychologist once said, "When you can no longer cry you have ceased to live." Sometimes a person who has known great unhappiness says, "I will never have faith again. I will build a wall around my life. Nothing will ever hurt me." These are strong words and, if lived, they mark the death of the individual.

When dreams die in a man's life his life is over. He is chained forever to the earth. Today one may witness a new birth of hope and faith in life, persons asking for a world of brotherhood. In the summer of 1968 I saw so many of these people, mostly teen-agers. They crowded the railroad stations in London, Amsterdam, Copenhagen, Oslo, Bonn, Stockholm, and Vienna. Many of these youngsters wore shirts and blue jeans and carried blanket rolls on their backs. They were visiting and talking to the children of men who have been traditional enemies of our people. They were saying, "Let us have and live in peace."

It was a sobering sight to see the Stars and Stripes flying in front of the University of Moscow, evidence of our students in study there. The young people have a dream, a dream that man will use his factories to produce not weapons but food and furniture and appliances, where money will not be used to destroy and kill but to feed and to educate and to build productive soils.

45

Someone said to me, "Why don't you tell it like it is?" I replied, "I know children get locked in jail, I know the ugly side of life, but I cannot tarry there. I must hurry to join the builders." Cynicism is a trademark of failure. We are surrounded on all sides by people who work to build a better world. They believe in the philosophy expressed in the sentence, "It is so human to look for the weakness in a man's life; it is so Christlike to look for the good."

The church has given us our institutions of higher learning. Our young people give up new cars, new clothes, spending money, to study in college and prepare themselves for the world they want to live in.

God is always near when a man stumbles. Civilization is a story of man's advancement in medicine, government, science, education, sociology, ecology, and faith. Why not make the promise to yourself today that you will join those who march to a better world?

I do not have to be rude because a man is rude to me. I do not have to be snobbish if my neighbor is or be a grouch if he is a grouch. I have no time to be negative. And so I must write of man's dreams, his triumphs, his search for love. I want to help him reach for a star. I have no other choice. You have no other choice, not really, because when God touches any one of us, we are lifted on wings, and we must reach because it is God's way.

Christmas
on the Farm

Behold, I bring you good tidings of great joy.—Luke 2:10

Christmas started in the one-room school. If you were one of the big boys the teacher sent you to the woods with an ax to bring back a fir tree. Time was found in the afternoon school program to string popcorn and cranberries for the fifteen-foot tree.

Do you remember the Christmas play? A wire was stretched across the front of the schoolroom and sheets were hung with safety pins for curtains. There were angels with halos and shepherds in bathrobes and readings and music. Kerosene lamps reflected a dreamy light over the festivities.

There was a Christmas tree at home too, draped with gold and silver tinsel. You worked hard to clip on the candle holders and insert the twisted pink, red, white, and green candles into the holders.

Christmas brought the family together. Breathlessly you waited to see if your brother made the long train trip back from Duluth, Minnesota. Members of the family arrived by horse and buggy, sometimes in a sleigh. Often your father drove to the station to meet an interurban or train, but by 1920 the Model T rattled up to the front door.

There are no words to describe the joy to a child's heart with the ringing of sleigh bells, the honking of an automobile horn, the bursting open of the door, the coming in of red-cheeked, laughing people with arms loaded with packages. Our hearts stood on tiptoe, for it was a great moment of joy. We were hugged and kissed. How good our aunt from Cincinnati smelled. How the house shook with laughter and talk and greetings so long suppressed.

The tree was barren underneath, but we knew, as children, there were stores of treasure hidden away— toys, candy, clothes which were to cover the floor under the tree the next morning as though Cinderella's fairy godmother had waved her magic wand.

You were permitted to get up early and go into the bedrooms and tug at the blankets with "Please get up!" Sometimes your Aunt Bess pulled you into bed with her and kissed you and gave you a big hug and said, "Don't pay any attention to Uncle Fred. He ought to be ashamed to tell you Santa Claus probably forgot to stop here."

There was always the question, "Shall we have breakfast first or open the presents?" Everyone knew what the answer would be. It was *our* day. You helped to pass out the presents in the midst of everyone's talking at once, "Oh, it is just what I wanted." "It fits perfectly. How did you know my size?" "I never expected to get one of these." You read all the names on the packages—who each package was for and who it was from. You laid the ones for you in the middle of the floor.

There was warmth and love, for we were together for such a short time. We felt a sadness in our hearts when the first to leave pulled on their coats and gloves, gathered their packages. Thanks for the memory of a wonderful childhood.

The Silent House

It is God that girdeth me with strength, and maketh my way perfect. —*Psalm 18:32*

Tonight you are sitting quietly in your easy chair reading or making things with your hands or just thinking. Memory is like an old rag doll, a worn chair, a ragged pair of pants, a faded shawl, symbols of yesterday.

On other nights it was not like this. Almost every minute of your time was demanded. The stairs were littered with toys and shoes. The dog raced through the kitchen after your son. Upstairs was the laughter of two girls. There was a scuffle to see who got to use the bathroom first for a shampoo. You settled that and hurried back down to take the cake out of the oven.

Later you sat and listened to homework. You patched a boy's pants while he read his history lesson. You signed a report card. You packed a lunch for a bike outing. You planned for Alice's tenth-year birthday party. There were so many busy moments. What a relief when the front door finally closed and everyone was off to school. The boisterous excitement of childhood seemed never to end.

Now that the door has closed on the children and they have homes of their own, you sit and think of the hugs and kisses, the excuses to prolong going to bed, the cry of illness in the night, and the excitement of going to the circus, the surprise birthday party, the first pony.

You open the letter again for the tenth time and read,

"My dearest Mother; I have just been appointed head resident physician at St. Luke's Hospital." You think about the telephone call from Paris: "Mother, after five weeks as secretary in the Paris embassy I am so happy. Let me tell you about the wonderful trip I had . . . ."

Darkness falls. You do not turn on the light. You hear the loud ticking of the clock. It never made so much noise before. There are no toys to pick up, no clothes to hang up. The house is spic and span. It stays that way. You close your eyes, and again in memory you see the pillow fights, the giggling, and "Mother, I am in bed." And later, "Mother, I'm thirsty." The countless little ways children have to get attention. Now you know it wasn't really a drink that was wanted, it was you. They loved you. They liked for you to fuss and make over them. They brought their cuts and scratches to you. They wept when you read from the Bible as their favorite Prince was laid to rest in the corner of the garden, knowing there would never be another dog like Prince.

And what excitement when they were off to college. The postman always kept you watching the mailbox for a letter. And so you bow your head and say, "Thank you, God, for the memory of my children. I am proud to have been a part of their lives."

And then the telephone rings, "Mother, we just arrived at the airport. We'll be home in fifteen minutes." Three grandchildren to spend the night with you! You hurry and get the beds ready.

A Stained-Glass Window

I am come a light into the world, that whosoever believeth on me should not abide in darkness.—John 12:46

I saw your name when I stepped into a church on Fifth Avenue one rainy afternoon. I read In Loving Memory of Betty Lynne Wellington which was etched into a small bronze plate beneath a stained-glass window.

In Loving Memory. These three words cover a life of eighty-four years. I felt your presence all about me. I remembered that you had started a fund, with your gift of a thousand dollars, for a new church organ. A young woman was practicing on the organ.

I left the church after the rain had ceased and walked joyfully down the avenue. I passed the children's day-care center. This had been your project too. A middle-aged man, Dr. William B. Wellington, came down the front steps. He is your son. You pounded a typewriter for eight years to help him have the money he needed for college and medical school. He is your gift to the world too.

Your daughter, Jean Ann, is a teacher. Your second son, Wilbur Ashley Wellington, is a New York composer. I see so much of you in your three children.

Betty Lynne Wellington, you have reached out with your heart, your mind, your hands, and your money with an influence that lives on and on. How fitting that your children and your friends made a tangible gift of a stained-glass window in your memory.

51

No one needs to be rich or even great, and certainly not famous, to give and to leave beauty in the world. The pennies and nickles that dribbled into collection plates through the years built cathedrals, established colleges, supported missions, constructed hospitals, cared for the poor. Wherever there is love one will find the church.

Betty Lynne Wellington was a warm woman. She brought a glow into the lives of people she touched. She had a way of drying the tears and bringing sunshine back into the hearts of the disturbed. You have walked the same road she walked. Have you forgotten that you have brought sunshine and hope into the lives of so many? If you have forgotten you may be sure that those you have helped along the way remember.

Sometimes a parent feels that the rearing of children today is so difficult. Betty Lynne Wellington never had much money, but she used the money she had to start great projects. Her enthusiasm drew others to do likewise. She believed in people. She believed in her children. She gave them more than just an opportunity to get an education. She taught them that God needed them to work in fields that would enrich human life.

There are so many Betty Lynne Wellington's in the world. As you read these words you must know that in this world the words *In Loving Memory* are engraved in the hearts of so many people who knew the love and beauty of your life.

An Old Fiddle

Therefore all things whatsoever ye would that men should do to you, do ye even so to them.   *—Matthew 7:12*

My name is Carl Keates. I remember you. I had a dream once, and you made it come true because you cared about people. When I was a boy in the twelfth grade I came to school one day with an old fiddle in a cotton flour sack. I had picked corn for two cents a bushel to buy the fiddle which was on display in a shop window for $14.85. It took me a long time to earn that money, and I remember how cold my fingers got with the snow heavy on the cornstalks.

I wanted to play in the high school orchestra. I was too poor to have music lessons. I was ashamed of the clothes I wore to school. I wasn't very welcome because all the orchestra members had private music lessons. I was tall, awkward, and shy, and I heard them whispering as I took the fiddle out of the flour sack.

You were my music teacher. You were kind and encouraging. You wanted every child in your classroom to have a chance, and you gave lessons after school. My fingers were so big I could not hold down a string. Always when I tried I held down two strings. Then one evening in late October you set up your music stand and laid on it handwritten sheets you had worked on for many nights. You wrote the complete music for me to play for the Thanksgiving program, using one finger on two strings.

The auditorium was packed that night of the program, and I was a part of the school orchestra. I was there because of you. I had scrubbed my hands and face and combed my hair again and again. My mother had ironed a shirt, and I had polished my heavy farm shoes the best that I could.

All I had to do was draw the bow across the strings at the right times. There was a song in my heart that night. When the concert was over, people came and shook my hand and congratulated me. There was a big lump in my throat because I remembered how helpless I had felt in the beginning and how you kept encouraging me to keep trying.

Why did you do this for me? You didn't have to go the second mile. You took a shy, faltering, stumbling boy, grown up too fast, and made it possible for him to be somebody that night of the concert. Do you understand why I remember you?

I last played at commencement. The old fiddle is here on a shelf. It reminds me of the night you shook my hand and told me how proud you were of me. I said that night that I was going to make something of my life because of the faith you had shown in me, and I have.

I know there are others like you—people who have said, "I believe in you." I have tried to pass on to others what you gave to me. Just an old fiddle, but a dream in the heart of a boy who wanted more in life than the labor of the fields. Thank you for giving me more.

Tied with Blue Ribbon

For where your treasure is, there will your heart be also.
—Matthew 6:21

In every heart are treasures of memory. I remember
the flash of the cardinal through the trees, the call of
the quail along the rail fence, the fragrant lilac in the
corner of the garden, the cool wind against my face.

But most of all I remember people. Walking in the
summer rain with you, the thrill of standing beside you
singing the school song, our laughter as we coasted
down a hill and tumbled into the snow.

You watched with me the shimmering moth against
the kitchen screen, listened with me to the owl far away
in the woods, lifted your eyes to the honking geese flying
south.

I remember the time you helped me with my algebra,
and the night we went ice skating; you baked cookies
for me when it was my birthday. I remember the red scarf
you used to wear around your throat and the soft hair
that curled about your face. Thank you for sharing a few
moments of childhood with me.

Treasures come in so many ways. A card in an old
scrapbook reminds me of the day we went on the Sunday school picnic. I took you boat riding on the lake
and the boat upturned. I thought you would never forgive me, and two days later came the card, and you had
written three words: "Wasn't it fun!"

I met you for the first time at compulsory chapel at

Earlham College. Your father was a Methodist preacher and you had had the advantage of voice lessons. I didn't know how to read notes, but I tagged along behind you. I remember best how pleasant it was to sit beside you.

Many of you are gone now. I think how good God has been to give us so many treasured moments with people. And I have known the joy of sometimes meeting again after many years, in the crowded department store, in a hospital room, at a college reunion, on a busy street. And we say, "Don't tell me. I remember your name."

I met you yesterday after twenty-five years of separation. It was at our college reunion. We walked endless miles over the campus and through the town talking over memories. You watched with me the colors of the evening sky, you held a white laden twig of blossoms I reached for you. You put your hands warmly against my cheeks and said good-bye before getting aboard your plane to go back home.

Somewhere in every life there may be a box with old letters tied with blue ribbon, but in every life there is a compartment in the heart filled with memories of happiness of the long ago.

Thank you, God, for the warmth that comes into our hearts when we read about the friends we used to know who contribute greatness to the world. Thank you for the hand that has held a child, the letter that comes on a special day, the constant reminder that love is the greatest thing in the world.

The Ugly Duckling

Give unto the Lord the glory due unto his name . . . worship the Lord in the beauty of holiness.

—I Chronicles 16:29

One of the most beautiful women I ever met was Eleanor Roosevelt. She was a warm woman. Her posture, her speech, her hands, all clearly revealed her kindness, her compassion, her unselfishness.

Some writers have said her voice was too high pitched, but I did not hear her voice, only her heart speaking for the neglected and the oppressed of the world.

As a young woman she was considered by some to be the ugly duckling of her socially prominent family. It must have been a great struggle for her to build a personality that would overcome her physical features.

Then one day she became a representative to the United Nations. So great was her contribution to this world organization that it honored her with a beautiful memorial on the grounds of the United Nations. The white marble memorial stands north of the rose gardens on the East River. The words on the memorial, "It is better to light a candle," speak well of the high esteem in which the world held her. In the National Archives Building one may read the letter sent to Eleanor Roosevelt by President Harry S. Truman. He refused to accept her resignation, because he could not replace her.

Everything about her was beautiful. Sometimes a girl says, "I am not pretty." I recall a student trip to Chicago many years ago. A girl who was shy and sensitive wanted to go, but I was afraid she might be left too much alone and be unhappy on the trip. A classmate, Darma Jean Monroe, spoke up: "I'll stay with her all the time on the trip. She will never be alone."

I shall always remember Darma Jean. It is the human heart that makes for beauty. This is true for so many people. It was a happy trip because the students were so considerate of one another. A wise man once said, "The only ugly thing in this world is what comes out of a man's mouth." He could have added that if we hold God close in our hearts, only kindness and love can come from us and spread to others.

In talking to Eleanor Roosevelt, I found her to be gracious, intelligent, interested in everyone. She was at the time I met her a noted writer, competent lecturer, and through the United Nations a champion of the underprivileged. She challenged the world to keep working for freedom from hunger, fear, the evils of slavery, to eradicate poverty and to educate for a better life. What she said may well remain a cornerstone for a better world for mankind.

Recently I walked through the Roosevelt mansion at Hyde Park. I was given a small tape recorder with a shoulder strap and a tape with the recorded voice of Eleanor Roosevelt. She described, as I walked from room to room, the home, its contents, its people. I felt I could reach out and touch her. Thank you, Eleanor Roosevelt, for showing us that if we are determined we can achieve in life.

I Think It's Spring

The desert shall rejoice, and blossom as the rose.
                                                —Isaiah 35:1

Sometimes you come into my store to buy some trivial thing. I hope you will come today; it is a cool and foggy morning. You moved into the green cottage down by the beach and came into my store one morning to buy some paint. I did not think that you were beautiful, but when you spoke I thought of spring.

I have known you in so many places, town and country. I met you in the subway. You smiled and said, "Take my seat." I met you in a flower shop with a pink bouquet of roses, and you said, "This is just what she would like."

When you talk I hardly move for fear that I will miss one soft accent, one golden word. I cherish the few moments you are in my store and envy those who share more hours with you. I look at your hands and want to touch them. They are rough and calloused like a gardener's, so beautiful. I was thrilled the afternoon you said as you were leaving my store, "Stop by sometime, and I'll show you my roses."

I followed you one balmy afternoon into a small paradise of color behind a stone wall, a wall standing as a barrier against the sea winds. The brick paths led past patterns of red and yellow and white. I remember the philosophy you shared with me, "The secret of a green thumb is getting down on your knees to plant and care for the garden children."

But what I remember most about that memorable afternoon was when I left you at the white board gate in the garden wall. You held out your hand to me, the hand I had wanted so long to touch. And when my hand touched yours I walked into a new dimension of life.

Did I say I did not find you beautiful until I heard you talk? Did I say that with your words spring came into my store? What is there left to say now that I have touched you? I looked long at you, before turning to go back to my store—your deep-set eyes, graying hair, wrinkled forehead, the unpressed dress you wore—and I saw a softness in the face kissed by the sun and the wind and the rain.

When you come into my store I am repaid for the hours I spend selling fish hooks, bread, boots, paint, and candy. I show you something new. I think of ways to keep you there. But always the screen door slams, and you are gone.

God, why did you give us friends who bring so much joy into our lives—the bricklayer, the musician, the poet, the restaurant cook, the bus driver, the chair maker, the postman? Why did you surround us with so many people who bring spring into our lives? Thank you, God.

The Stars
Will Remember

My cup runneth over.   *—Psalm 23:5*

You never wanted me to be a perfect person. You saw in me only a worthy human being. And because God filled your life with so much beauty he led you to a path that crossed mine. You saw that I was lonely, a human being worthy of being touched. And so you loved me.

How did you know that my shoulders were bent beneath a burden that I could not overcome alone? Was it your loving hand, God? Did he whisper into your hand and say, "Here is a person who needs your understanding and your strength"?

And so we walked a winding lane. The stars were in the sky. There was the smell of new-mown hay and the night calls of life. I reached out and took your hand. You did not seem to mind. You were glad that our spirits met. We walked for hours, and you listened as I opened the secret place of my heart and let you in. No one had ever been there before. I had carried my burden alone. I felt your hand tighten in mine. I knew you understood.

We paused before a lazy, drifting stream. There were a thousand stars reflected in the waters. We were alone in the world, far away from the noise and the chatter of the streets. Just the two of us. Then you lifted your face to me and said softly, "You may kiss me."

For a moment I held your softness in my arms. I felt

the beating of your heart against mine. I felt the strength of your arms. And then you turned and swiftly vanished down the path.

I am not old, but my hair is gray, and my heart has learned to reach out to others when I am lonely as you reached out to me in the long ago. I have learned to live within the love of God's all-understanding heart. Sometimes I see the scar of yesterday's hurt. Sometimes I remember.

The path is walked tonight by other lovers and the stars have not changed. I walk alone, but when I look up I say, "Stars, do you remember when she walked this path with me? Do you remember her parting words?"

Yes, the stars remember. The world has forgotten, but the stars remember. "I will love you until the end of time." I hear you call my name, and I walk tall tonight because of you. Sometimes I wonder where you are, what you are doing, if you ever think of me. And then I remember that through these years you have always walked beside me. I forget that God reached out and took you, and you cannot come back to me in person.

Sometimes it is not easy, but I cannot question God who gave us life, gave us each other. I know that someday I shall walk down this path for the last time as you did. Then my spirit will merge with your spirit, and we shall be together forever.

I feel the soul within me tugging to be free. I hear you whisper, God, "Wait a little longer. My hand is upon you. I have work yet for you to do. Be patient. The cup that I have given you leads to eternal life."

The Second Mile

And whosoever shall compel thee to go a mile, go with him twain.   *—Matthew 5:41*

Courage can be found in so many places. Often you walk the second mile with others. Do you walk the second mile with yourself?

Thousands of people across the nation enroll in night school. Their ages are from seventeen to seventy, and if they have completed the eighth grade they must go two nights a week, three hours a night for eight years to get a high school diploma.

Listen as a teacher speaks the first night. "You people work eight hours a day in the factory, at the grocery check-out counter, in the home. You go home, get the evening meal, sometimes arrange for a baby-sitter, and then you have nerve enough to come down here and study for three hours. I salute you!"

You will notice Ethel Riggin when you first step into the classroom. She is immaculate, a woman of forty-seven, back in school for the first time in thirty-four years. She was married at thirteen, had her three children by the time she was eighteen, and now has her own business and five grandchildren.

Tom Higgins is forty-two years of age. He has a small car-repair shop. He has two children in Indiana University. Both of them are honor-society members. He promised them that he would get a high school education. He dropped out of high school twenty-six years ago to help support his mother and eight younger brothers, following the death of his father.

Ruth Bowen pounds the typewriter all day to keep her daughter in college. It takes all her husband's small salary to keep their family of three children who are still at home.

Fred Dickerson is a farm boy. He will graduate this spring. His father owned a big farm and kept Fred out of school so much that he quit school at the end of his freshman year. When he came back to school he could not write or spell. He had difficulty in speaking. His wife tutored him at home, and it will be a proud night in the family's life when he puts on his cap and gown.

Betty Benson will graduate in one more year. She was born into a family of twelve children. Her parents gave her away because they could not feed so many mouths. Her aunt worked her as a servant in the home. Betty escaped at seventeen to marry a man who is devoted to her. After the three children came she made a promise to go back to school.

None of these people could have gone back to school and been successful without the backing of the home— kids that did the dishes, a husband or wife that gave them time to study at home. One never forgets graduation night when children, grandchildren, neighbors turn out to welcome the adult graduate.

Sometimes achievement comes by traveling a long and hard road. Thank you for helping.

I Have a Friend
Up There

A friend loveth at all times.   *—Proverbs 17:17*

A few days ago I was pushing a hospital patient in a wheelchair to the physical therapy department. The woman made this comment: "I am going to cheer up the kids down there and tell them some funny stories."

Her hair was neatly combed, and she had on soft green slippers and a velvet gown. Her warm heart was a real part of her. She said to me, "I am ninety-six years years old."

I put one hand on her shoulder and said, "Bless you."

Then she told me the story of her life. "The Lord told Peter to feed his sheep. I have been doing that all my life. I made up my mind many years ago that the devil loves a cross, cranky old woman. I didn't want the devil to love me. I wanted God to love me. And I knew that I could best win his love by loving others."

When I brought her back to her room I put both my hands on her shoulders and wished her a happy trip home. She took my hand, held it against her face, and said, "Thank you."

Long after, I thought of how greatly she enriched my thinking. I am not supposed to talk to a patient, and above all, not touch a patient. Had I wheeled her silently to therapy and back, I would never have learned the wonderful lesson I did from her.

She said, "I have a friend up there." I had never

thought of it quite like this. She wasn't complaining about her pains, her shaking legs, her advanced years. She was thinking of others. She did kid the wonderful, wonderful young men and women who do the therapy work. I marvel at the joy they bring to the patients who come to them. Theirs is a work of love.

When I see an orderly gently lifting and turning a patient in bed or hear a choir singing "He Lives" or thrill to the robin's early morning song, then I understand the man up there who says, "Go love my people—feed them."

You can stay young in heart always. Let God love you, not the devil, by being the kind of person God wants you to be. For just twenty-four hours try to live with joy in your heart. Promise that you will not say one word to hurt another, but you will praise and lift and push with all your might to help others bring out the best that is within them. People all about you want to express joy. Give them a chance. Put the old negative type of thinking behind you and become a positive person.

Yes, you have a friend up there. And he says to you each morning, "This is a new day to be glad. Let joy be in your heart." You will draw people to you. There is something about a joyful spirit that lights up the world. Let your light shine as did that of the elderly woman who saw not only beauty and joy in the world but fun too. Learn to laugh again if you have forgotten. There are so many waiting to laugh with you.

I Didn't Know
You Cared, God

My God, my God, why hast thou forsaken me?
—Matthew 27:46

No one can escape the darkness of life. We used to sing in the little country church a song that went like this: "Back of the clouds the sun is always shining." My mother taught this song to me. We were riding home one night in a buggy, and a severe storm came up. My sister and I cried, not because we were afraid but because we thought the rain would spoil a picnic planned for the next day. My mother explained the need the earth had for water. And she said, "Always the sun is shining back of the clouds." This lesson has followed me through life.

The Son of God was called a man of sorrows. This name was given to him because he devoted most of his life to healing the sick, feeding the poor, encouraging the lonely and the sad, reaching out to a world that was filled with grief.

But Jesus laughed. He had his happy moments. Sometimes we cry over small things: we didn't get the bicycle we wanted for our birthday; we lose a football game; we have to miss a birthday party because we are ill.

Sometimes we reach out for God, and we cannot find him. We say, "Why did God let this happen? Why did he do this to me?" We feel so helpless to understand.

Phillip Commons lay for many days in intensive care with a tube in his neck. He thought he was going to die, but he did not want to die because he had work to do. He asked God to spare him because other people needed him. God answered his prayer.

Phillip Commons tells this story. "I thought God had passed me by. I lost my job when the company I worked for went out of business. I was fifty-two, and there wasn't another business in the city like the one I had worked for. Then one Sunday after I had been out of work for several weeks a friend stepped up to me at church and asked me how I would like to work in personnel. He told me he needed a man like me, someone who could work with people and understand their problems. At fifty-two it was the first job I ever had that I was really happy doing. What a break."

When Phillip Commons went home from the hospital to recover he was overwhelmed by the gifts of food, the cards, the callers, men and women and children whose families he had helped in personnel. He realized that people loved him because he had become involved in their lives, helping them iron out their money problems, their family problems, planning for further education.

God does care. He never promised that we would not walk in darkness. He never said life would be easy. He never said we would not suffer. But he said he loved us, and the yoke would be light because he would walk with us.

Yes, God does care. He reaches out to us in so many different ways. Sometimes we find ourselves laughing through our tears. God gave us laughter. It is like the sun, leaving the darkness behind.

There Is No Death

He that believeth in me, though he were dead, yet shall he live: And whosoever liveth and believeth in me shall never die.   —John 11:25-26

Sometimes a minister is asked this question: "What do you say when you call at a funeral home and meet someone who has lost someone very dear to them?" The answer is really simple. Sometimes you don't say anything. Your presence, the touch of hands, the eyes, all say, "I understand."

In a funeral home recently there was a line of people waiting to express sympathy to the family. A child of about five years was holding her father's hand tightly. She looked up at her father, stood on tiptoe, and her father reached down and picked her up. How happy and comfortable she looked in his arms, the arms of a father she loved.

Love is a word. You cannot draw a picture of it. You cannot give it color or form. Sometimes it can withstand neglect, time, distance, and heartache. When Jesus hung on the cross he understood man's desire to live. His last words to the thief upon the cross were words of forgiveness. "Because I live ye too shall live. This day you will be with me in paradise," he said.

There are many chapters in a person's life. We are not sure when one ends and another begins. It is unfortunate that many times we remember only the suffering of a loved one. But every person was at one time a young boy or girl, perhaps skipping across the fields with

69

a dog, looking at the blue sky, listening to the birds, eager to explore and understand God's wonderful world of color. Then there is a period of school, a time of marriage, a time of middle age. As we look back on these periods of life we find that many times there is a period of darkness between each period.

In a real sense we die each night. We are not conscious; we lose contact with the world. In a sense we experience a resurrection each time we awake. Yet we have no fear of going to sleep. When we awaken the tiredness of the body is gone. We open our eyes to beauty again. We are back in a world of reality.

Men die like this. The difference is that they awaken in a world that is not the earth. Many years ago a program was taken into the schools by the Moody Bible Institute. Pictures were shown of the miracle of the unfolding of flowers. Students were told that there are thousands of "Earths" out there on which people live. We are sometimes unwilling to accept the world in which we live. We do not understand the life of a plant any more than we understand the life of a person. We do not know what makes the heart beat. We do know that all humanity yearns for eternal life and that this yearning is God-given. Jesus had no reason to tell men that they shall live forever except that it is so.

Cathedral of Trees

With God all things are possible.   *—Mark 10:27*

Shirley Medford tells the story of her first trip to California: "We were traveling up the highway past towns, houses, cars, people, not unlike travel in any state. Then we entered northern California and were soon on the Avenue of the Giants. After our car was parked I walked into the woods.

"There in the silence I looked up and up and up. Could there really be trees like the 'big trees'? Or was it my imagination? I felt the presence of God all around me. I had never had quite the feeling I had as I stood in the cathedral of trees.

"Then I looked up again, and I prayed to God a prayer of joy. I thanked God for giving me eyes to see, to see the soft greens and browns of these giants that were born as long ago as Christ.

"I had seen Bryce Canyon. I had looked upon the great expanse of the Grand Canyon. I had traveled through sunburned deserts. I had watched the endless flow of the tides on the Pacific coast. But the trees were different. In the majestic silence of the unspoiled beauty I felt I had stepped into another world. The forest floor was alive with plants creeping across the moist rich earth, some reaching up for a flicker of sunlight, some with small white flowers.

"Sometimes I feel like the white flower. I am not

71

very big. God does things on a grand scale—the sunrise, the blue sky, the rains, the warm breath of spring over the countryside. He seems to be in full control of them. I seem small beside God's world, but I know he loves me. He breathes life into the tiny plants living at the foot of the cathedral giants. He breathes life into me. But I do not understand what life is. He does. And so I am not afraid of death, because he understands this too.

"The cathedral plants hold the soil around the roots of the great giants when the storms come. Maybe I sometimes just happen to be in the right place when the storms come into the lives of people I love. And because I am there they are able to walk and live again.

"Dear God, I feel so small beside the towering trees. But I am glad because I feel your greatness. I know that you love me as you love your trees. I know that I am the sparrow Jesus talked about. I know that you love me. Thank you, God, for loving me.

"We have only to see the world about us and then we know what the Bible means when it talks about the earth proclaiming your glory, God. Thank you because you included us in your kingdom. It is a comfort to know that you call us your children.

"I shall never forget when I stood on holy ground so close to you, God, in the cathedral of trees."

My Wonderful America

Greater love hath no man than this, that a man lay down his life for his friends. —*John 15:13*

I have seen your children stand before the Tomb of the Unknown Soldier. They stand in silence watching the change of the guard.

I have seen your children reach out and touch the Liberty Bell in Independence Hall in Philadelphia, a touch of reverence for what the bell stands for.

I have seen your children look upon the Declaration of Independence and the Constitution of the United States in the National Archives building.

I have seen your children looking up at the towering figure of Abraham Lincoln in the Lincoln Memorial.

Your children! It is a memory now, the twenty-eight trips I made to Washington and New York with your children as a senior sponsor. It is a simple but wonderful thing to say that we have the finest generation of boys and girls in the two hundred years of this nation.

Do not permit the front page of the newspaper to hide the fact that you mothers and fathers and teachers have done a work pleasing to God. You have helped children to understand and appreciate the great democracy in which they live.

Thousands of boys laid down their lives to preserve the freedom of this nation. Its future is in the hands of our children. I remember my last trip with these high school seniors. As our boat came close to the Statue of Liberty I told them the story of 1947 when I stood on the deck of the *Queen Elizabeth* and wept because I was returning to my country, the land I love.

My wonderful America. You have reached out your arms to the world. You have given again and again. You have never asked anything in return, only that the peoples of the world might have food and hospitals and education and freedom in government. You have wanted other peoples in other lands to live and enjoy their cultures as we love ours. You have been so generous.

My wonderful America. I see you in the restaurant, on the trains, in the stores, the streets. I see your flag in every classroom. You are the heartbeat of opportunity. You are the heartbeat of freedom. A lump comes into my throat when I see the Stars and Stripes flying in the breeze. I know what this flag means—my right to worship you, God. My right to speak, to live where I want to live, to work where I want to work.

Sometimes I ask what I have done to deserve living in the land I love so much. Perhaps if I helped a few boys and girls to understand and love you, then I have done what I could.

My wonderful America. Each night I thank God that I was fortunate enough to be born under your flag. May I always cherish the freedom you have given me.

Frank Guyatt Speaks

Let your speech be alway with grace, seasoned with salt,
that ye may know how ye ought to answer every man.
—Colossians 4:6

Frank Guyatt is a clergyman, world traveler, public speaker, who has inspired thousands of boys and girls in our high schools to believe in themselves and in the United States of America. For many years he has filmed the Olympic games, and he sees in the youth of today the hope of tomorrow.

A few weeks ago I visited Frank Guyatt in the intensive-care of the hospital. He had a tube in his throat and could not speak. He was critical for many days. I could not stop the prayer in my heart because God would not let me. God didn't let him lose his voice. God didn't let him die. But Frank Guyatt knows that it was the prayers reaching out to him that gave him life.

God reaches out so often through us. We do walk in darkness sometimes. We do face problems. But the key to walking back into the sunshine, the secret of recovering from a deep illness, is found in a letter that Frank Guyatt wrote: "How can I ever thank you for your many visits, your prayers and just being there. The card you sent me was so expressive of your sincere love. Thanks and ever again my thanks for your thoughtfulness."

You can't thank people. You don't have to. The gift you give is often so important, so big, there are no words other than *thank you*. How many times have you stood as a giant, been there at the right moment, said the right word? You expect no reward. You expect no one to pay you back. You gave because you could.

And you have said again and again as people thank you, "Why, I did just what anyone else would have done." If you believe this then you must believe that when you walk through a dark night there are voices out there praying for you. Listen, and you will hear them.

It is not easy to hold the attention of high school youngsters today. They are so active, so much on the go. But when Frank Guyatt flashes on the screen his pictures of the hundreds of boys and girls of every nation showing their skills, the sportsmanship, the good feeling, the giving of their best, high school youngsters sit up and notice.

Once at the end of the picture he showed the Stars and Stripes flying, and he said, "This is your flag. For two hundred years it has stood for freedom and opportunity. Don't ever do anything to bring it down to the earth. Keep it flying for all the world to see. This morning you young people share in the finest educational system in the world."

"What do you charge for showing your pictures?" Frank Guyatt was once asked. "My biggest payment is watching the attentive boys and girls showing pride in the great efforts put forth by our American athletes."

Bloom Where You Are

The desert shall rejoice, and blossom as the rose.
—Isaiah 35:1

Carrie Robbins is a name that brings to those who knew her the word *beautiful*. This was the kind of life she lived. Her nature was sweet and gentle, and she was wise and kind. It was a privilege to walk through her front door and sit in her spacious living room and feel the challenge for living. Her zest for life never dimmed even in the remaining days of her life when she knew that she was slowly dying. She never carried a candle. Her own light was a bright one.

You will find Carrie Robbins living in your town. She is to be found everywhere. She is a loyal friend with devotion to her family, an undying faith in God, and insurmountable courage. You will find her living on your street.

Someone said of Carrie Robbins, "She gave enthusiastic support for wholesome and benevolent activities, replacing words with deeds, criticism with understanding. The welfare of her church was her constant concern. She faced adversity bravely, firmly believing that overcoming problems increased strength. With her kind thoughts and her hands she left beauty where she passed because she blessed the lives she touched."

Look carefully at yourself in a mirror. You may be a Carrie Robbins. She lived in a small town of less than two thousand residents. She was strongly supported in her faith by her husband, Earl Robbins, who was a Sunday school teacher and a small-town attorney who forgot to send statements to widows for legal work.

Many times we say, "I can't do that. Get someone else." Carrie Robbins said, "I will." Why do we insist on trying to convince ourselves that other people can do a better job? Why do we sometimes think we are a nobody?

Jesus chose his disciples from men who lived around him. He knew that within their minds, hearts, and souls was the capacity to grow. You have this same capacity to grow.

Elizabeth Lashley was a lifelong teacher who never married. She never left the small town where she was born. Among her possessions was a framed note that read, "I am sending you flowers on this Mother's Day for the hundreds of boys and girls whose lives you guided into greatness." Truly they were all her children. She did what she could.

In every little town across the nation and in the country on isolated farms are great people who have chosen to bloom where they are. These people have made and are making great contributions to the community about them. Count carefully the contributions that you are making to life, and let your heart be full of joy.

Song of the Sea

Wherever this gospel is preached in the whole world,
what she has done will be told in memory of her.
                                        —Matthew 26:13 RSV

This is the story of a woman, her name unknown, who did a service for Jesus. Perhaps you have felt as he did when someone reached out to you with love. And you have said, "Why are you doing this for me?"

Across the years, so many years, came a card recently from a person who had vanished in the past. I think the one who sent the card saw my name in the alumni magazine.

I read the letter many times, and then I went out walking on the beach where we had walked so many years before. One does not really ever forget. The soft waters came racing up about my feet, then restlessly rolled back into the sea as if by a powerful force. The sea had not changed, not in centuries of time. But we change. We had walked along this beach thirty years before. We were young then, with the vision of youth. We could do all things as we reached for a dream. How many other couples have walked this same beach! Dear God, you fill our lives with hopes and dreams and visions of success. We have not really lived, have we, until we have shared a thousand tears in broken dreams, a thousand moments of extreme joy? Too soon the night is gone and morning comes.

I look out over the great expanse of water to where it meets the sky. The waters say to me, "I go on and on, never ending. So it is with your life. You will never die. God has work for you to do, no matter how humble. Believe in him. He will show you the way."

And now I am listening to memories of the night we walked along the beach. You helped me grow into a mature, loving person. I think how poor I might have been had you not touched my life. The waves washed away your footprints on the sands of so many years ago, but never in my heart. I see your smile; I feel your touch; I hear your words. I stand tall because of you.

The song of the sea is adventure. It calls to boys and girls everywhere. They fill the college classrooms, the laboratories, seeking the knowledge to become the leaders in a new world. It will be their world, hopefully a world they will want. But the sea goes on. It never changes. The footprints are washed away because we can never go back. A higher power is calling, calling us in every generation to lay aside the schoolbooks and pick up the tools of life.

When I read your card I was reminded of the thirty years of service you have rendered as a nurse. It was there that God called you. It was a long journey from the sands by the sea to the hospital room. But God went with you.

I Came to See You

The flowers appear on the earth; the time of the singing of birds is come, and the voice of the turtle is heard in our land.   —*Song of Solomon 2:12*

A small girl of about nine years walked into my flower garden one sunny morning. A cardinal sang from high in a cottonwood tree, the fragrance of freshly opened sweet peas filled the air, and this beautiful child added to the beauty of the garden.

"Pretty flower," she exclaimed as she bent over to smell a hearty pink carnation. She touched a long-stemmed dark purple larkspur and stroked the petals of a yellow rose, tripping from one flower to another with many an "oh-h" at each discovery.

I held back the words I was about to say. The words I wanted to speak were, "Oh, my garden is so weedy. You should have seen it last week. I cut my finger Monday and couldn't pull weeds, and the rain makes the weeds grow so fast."

The truth given to us by a child is so simple. She was looking at flowers, not weeds. She was seeing that which was beautiful. I was seeing weeds, and she was seeing flowers.

Our worst enemy sometimes is a negative mind. We worry about our mistakes. We do not take time to be thankful for the good we say and do.

A few days ago I called at a home without announcing that I was coming. In the old days, by the time a minister got out the halter and tied his horse to the hitching post and got to the front door a woman had time to put on a fresh apron and straighten her hair. I found Mrs. Harris on a stepladder washing the top sash of her south living room window. She was in her stocking feet, there was a black streak across her face, and she wore a soiled apron.

"Oh, I wasn't expecting company. I look a sight. And my house! I haven't done my breakfast dishes, but you may come in. I'm ashamed to ask you in. You'll think I'm a poor housekeeper." She climbed down from the stepladder and led me around to the front door.

"Mrs. Harris," I explained, "I didn't come to see your kitchen. I know you have to clean house like everyone else. I know dishes have to be washed. But, I didn't come to see what kind of housekeeper you are, I came to see you."

A few minutes later I had a cup of chocolate in my hand, and Mrs. Harris and I were talking about the Sunday school picnic. We were warm friends exchanging ideas about the wonderful world in which we live. The dirty dishes in the kitchen were forgotten. I mentioned the purple and white flowers in the picture over the piano. Mrs. Harris had painted the picture. I talked about the border of flowers along the drive. She had spent hours to make it so attractive and pleasing to all who drove by her house. All at once she was happy and aware that someone saw the beauty she had created.

Do Not Be Afraid

Master, Master, we perish. . . . And he said unto them,
Where is your faith? —*Luke 8:24-25*

I was so tired, God, when I went to bed last night.
My arms and legs could hardly move. This morning I
am no longer tired. I am ready for a new day.

I was so hungry when I got up. The warm toast and
butter and rolled oats filled me, and the orange juice
was refreshing.

I was so unhappy when I found the rabbits had gone
down my row of lettuce in the garden. Then my neighbor came over and said, "I've got bushels of lettuce. Let
me give you all you can eat. Yours will grow again."

I was so discouraged when my car stopped running
two miles from home. It was so unnecessary for me to
run out of gas. You pulled up and said, "I have a can
with two gallons of gas. Enough to get you home."

I was afraid as I stood on the curb in Chicago. You
said, "Let me take your arm and help you across this
busy street. I am used to the city."

I was so hungry when you knocked at my door and
said, "Come and go to church with me this evening."
You knew my hunger to be with someone and to worship again.

I was so puzzled about life until I sat down beside you
on a bus going into town. You gave me a little white
booklet and told me you were giving it away to people
everywhere. I thanked you, and that night I read *The*

Story of the Christmas Guest which you had given to me on the bus. Helen Steiner Rice tells the story from an old German legend. It is about a shoe cobbler who dressed his shop in branches of fir at Christmas because the Lord had appeared to him in a dream and said he would come for a visit. But all that came were an old beggar, a tired old woman, and a lost child.

I don't think I will ever be unhappy or lonely again. Between you, God, and friends, I won't have much chance. It seems that everyone in the world cares about me. I know, God, that it is you who restore the broken heart, the tired body. I know it is you who bring beauty. When I walked out this morning and saw the brightly opened flowers by my door they seemed to shout to me, "Here I am! I am the Lord, thy God. Look upon my beauty for it is mine. I created it for you, my children. It is your garden of flowers, your earth. I give it to you because I love you. Because you are mine."

Yesterday I was afraid, but I will never be afraid again, because I see life today through different eyes. I hear the laughter of children in the yard. I felt soft drops of rain on my face this morning. I answered the telephone and the first words were, "I wanted to talk to you." And then the voice said, "I want to thank you." All at once I am alive again. Dear God, thank you for lifting me and helping me to see again.

What Is a Child Worth?

And the woman conceived, and bare a son: and when she saw him that he was a goodly child, she hid him three months. And when she could not longer hide him, she took for him an ark of bulrushes. —*Exodus 2:2-3*

"She's gorgeous! She's ours! And we love her!"

These words came over the radio a few days ago from a woman who had just received a child from a war-torn world. She did not pick the child from an orphanage or take it from a welfare department. The baby was one of several hundred flown in by air, and it was laid in her arms. It is not easy to brush away the tears of joy when the future of this little girl can be seen in a home where there is love and security.

When a man loses his job because a machine takes over or war breaks up a family, it is the children who suffer. Thousands of children have the chance for a new life because childless homes open up to them. Above the din of war and destruction the human heart reaches up and up to you, God.

What is a child worth? Must it be hungry and ill-dressed while fathers stand in picket lines? Must there always be man against man? Can we see man's slow climb to build the better world he yearns for? Give us patience, God, give us understanding, give us a forgiving love.

We do not have to go to faraway places to find the needy. They are all around us. We are mindful of them. They come to our schools. We give them free lunches, we clothe them. We give them scholarships for college. We say that no child in this nation who has the ability shall be denied an education.

We understand what dignity means to a man, a chance to help himself. And it is from our hands, from our labor, that we share with those who have needs.

I stood on a college campus not long ago congratulating a young man who had received a fellowship to study in Europe. He said to me, "I want you to meet my mother and my father." There was pride and an adoring love in his voice as he presented his parents to me. He knew and I knew that when his parents died in an automobile accident when he was only six months old, a couple went to the welfare department and said, "We want that baby." For twenty-three years he had lived in an atmosphere of devoted love from the foster parents. And I think he was proud of himself that day because he had made them proud of him.

I hear America calling, "Give us a child to love and care for." They are waiting because there are not enough unfortunate children to go around. Our children are all we have that really belong to us. The great American heart does not recognize race or color. When a plea comes to feed the hungry child somewhere in the world, we give. And we are aware of what one man said: "We can give a child a cup of water, but we need to ask why he is thirsty."

In My Garden

And the Lord God planted a garden.　　　　*—Genesis 2:8*

They say it is my garden, but I only own the ground. I remember your saying to me, "Wait until I get a spade, I want to give you a start of my Shasta daisies." I planted them in the corner of my garden.

The spirelike flowers of my blue delphinium are tied back, but I still have to duck when I go through my garden gate. You brought them to me one fall from a nursery in Fairfax County near Washington.

You knocked on my back door one evening and held up a vine. "I had a sprout of my silver lace vine. You must have one." That fall, airy sprays of thousands of silvery white flowers bloomed, but the winter was hard, and the vine froze to the ground. The next winter it survived, and when I went out one warm June morning I found the catbird had built a nest in a fork.

"I want to give you something to remember me by," you said. You called it a resurrection plant. I planted it by the garden wall. It came up with a cluster of green leaves. Then the leaves died, and I said that I must plant something else there to take its place. But before I got to it, I walked into my garden one morning, and there they stood, the tall purple lily flowers that had come up overnight. These flowers come back every summer, and I think of you.

I tried for years to get a start of the lily of the valley

but in vain. One day you brought me a start and you said, "You don't plant them in the right place. Here, let me show you." I have so much to learn about flowers. I know now that no two are alike. Each flower requires a special kind of care.

I walk down my garden path when friends come to see me. It is a conversation piece. In almost every flower I see a person who wanted to share with me. What greater material gift can one give than a flower?

My ever-blooming hollyhocks are my pride and joy. You said I ought to have some. I said they take up so much room. But you handed me some seeds and told me to try them. Now from July to October I have a rainbow of color, pink, red, white, yellow, and orange. My garden would not be complete without them.

I think what I love most of all are the hearty primrose plants that almost push up through the snow. You said your mother always grew them in England and that American gardens liked them too. I like them because they are the first to bloom in the spring.

One of my prize plants is a dandelion. A child brought it to me one day because of the huge two-inch golden bloom. A cloudburst had washed it out of a hillside, and I have kept it in memory.

They say it is my garden, but this really is not true. I only own the ground; the flowers belong to you.

A Handful of Stones

*A new commandment I give unto you, That ye love one
another; as I have loved you.   —John 13:34*

He who destroys another person with his tongue does
not love. Sometimes in our weakness we do this. Hanging
in the United Nations is a great tapestry. The guide will
tell you that there is one flaw in the weaving. The weav-
ers did this on purpose because they believed that only
God is perfect.

If you hold a stone in your hand you cannot shake
your neighbor's hand. You must first drop the stone. Jesus fully understood man's envy, hatred, malice, and
jealousy. In simple, humble words he presented to man
a vision of God's kingdom where evil did not exist. Jesus
knew the nature of man's thinking.

But Jesus also understood man's dream to be better,
his vision of a more beautiful life, of wanting to be ac-
cepted and loved. He illustrates this in the story of the
woman taken in adultery. It was the custom to take a
woman so condemned to the outskirts of the city and
there to further shame her by stripping her clothes away
and stoning her until she died. He saw in this woman a
hope that he could help her to a better life. If he had
not pardoned her, then the lives of all who lived after
her would have been without hope, for without forgiveness there is no life.

There are many ways to destroy a human life, ways
other than stones and guns. The human tongue is a

deadly weapon, and Christians need to be aware that in their zeal to uphold the ethics of Jesus they remember his commandment to love and to forgive. We may not envy the thief upon the cross. He was paying for his crime. But when he begged for mercy Jesus heard him, and Jesus granted his plea. We, then, need to be sure that our hearts are filled with love when our time comes to pray to God.

Life is never easy. We suffer emotional, mental, and physical pain. We know what it is to have dreams that die. We know what it is to cry on our pillow at night. We know what it is to have others ignore us. We know what it is to be rejected. But Jesus will not leave us. He makes us uncomfortable. He stands at our side. He says that we are to go the second mile, to give our cloak away. He asks us to be aware of those who hunger, those who thirst, and those who are naked. He promises us peace in our hearts if we follow him.

A handful of stones. Can we drop them? Can we extend a hand and say, "I want to help lift your burden. At first I did not understand you because you were not like me. You were of a different color. You spoke a different language. You wore different clothes. But now I know that you are a person, a person worthy of being loved. God gave you life. I am dropping the stones from my hands. I offer you my friendship. I do this because I love you."

Janet Weller

Were there not ten cleansed? but where are the nine?
There are not found that returned to give glory to God,
save this stranger. —*Luke 17:17-18*

How wonderful it is to walk on tiptoe through heaven, to feel that we have helped another person to have a happy day, that the warmth of our life has spread into the life of another.

Richard Collins tells this story: "I stopped in a supermarket one evening. While I was selecting some ice cream, a lovely young woman stepped up and spoke to me. She had been a student in psychology when I taught six years before. I remember her words.

" 'Hello, Mr. Collins. Do you remember me? I was with some of the girls last evening, and we were talking about you. We remember so many things you taught us. I know there were times when you thought we weren't paying much attention to what you said in class. Every morning when we came into your room we looked up at the blackboard to see what thought you had written there for the day. I think the one I remember best was "Give to the world the best you have, and the best will come back to you."

" 'You remember Alice Morey? She was at our get-together last night. She said, "I wasn't very pretty, and I wasn't the smartest girl in class, but Mr. Collins always treated me like a person, like everyone else." I guess that is the reason we all loved you. We think so often of the things you said to us. We always felt safe and secure in your classroom.' "

Richard Collins made this comment: "Sometimes I have said to someone 'You've made my day.' Well, Janet Weller, you've made my next ten years."

There are many Richard Collinses everywhere. When a person retires he often wonders what contribution he has made to life. You will not have to think deeply to recall the times when you have felt the glow within you as you think of the people your smile, your touch have lifted.

There is an old saying that we can give without loving, but we cannot love without giving. All about us are people who have needs. One of man's greatest needs is to have someone to believe in him. This knowledge made Jesus Christ a popular person. He understood the weakness in a man's life, but he never failed to see the hope in a man's heart to be better than he was. Each day, whether you are aware of it or not, you touch another's life. He may tell you about it in ten years or never at all. We are sometimes like the nine lepers. Jesus helped them. He opened a new life for them. Of course they were grateful, but the new life before them was so promising they just forgot to say thanks to the man who gave them life.

There are many Janet Wellers in the world, the people who come back and say "Thank you for helping me to establish values in life."

God Is Everywhere

He that heareth my word, and believeth on him that sent me, hath everlasting life. —*John 5:24*

I heard you call my name. And I was no longer alone. You pushed open my front door and came over by the warmth of my fireplace. Your presence was like the morning sun pushing up over the purple hills. I felt a joy flooding my heart because you had come. You looked at the clay pot of scarlet geraniums on the windowsill. Your fingers touched the leaves, and you told me how beautiful the plant was. What you were really saying was that I am a good flower grower. And this made me happy.

Do you remember, God, when the first blossom opened? I looked up and said, "Welcome, God, into my house this morning."

Sometimes I become weary waiting for the spring to come. My hands are growing rusty from not digging in the soil. I find myself going to the window to look into the gray skies. I return to my fireplace and my book. I wanted to say hello to the postman, but he came without my knowing. I had a glimpse of him going down the sidewalk leaving a trail of white steam from his lips in the frosty air. He left a few advertising folders and from among them a card fell into my lap, a card with small handwriting. With shaking hands I open it wondering who it is from, what joy it will bring, what memories it will stir.

The card is from you, written late one Sunday evening from Portland. You thought about me. And you signed the card "Forever." One word, *forever,* and your name. I sit looking into the fire, thinking of the meaning of that word, recalling our childhood and times together. I know the word *forever* means that you are my friend, that you understand me, and that you love me.

I sat in the fourth row of the church this morning. You have been our minister only a short time. I like you, and I like to be close to you when you talk. Your voice is strong and convincing and comforting. I say to myself, "It is God who is speaking. He is using you as a channel of his love." Your heart is understanding, and we are happy when we talk to you. We know we can open our hearts to you; our sorrows, our hopes, and our dreams we can share with you. Thank you for being our friend.

When I was in my yard this morning you came running into my arms because you were afraid. I held you close to me and told you the dog just wanted to be friends, and we petted him together. There is so much for a child to learn, but you made me feel strong and important that I could help you brush away your fears. It is so good to be needed.

Dear God, how many times a day do I run into your arms because I am afraid, because I love you, because I know you understand me. Thank you, God, for touching my life when my neighbor comes in, when the postman brings me a letter, when you speak to me from the pulpit, and in the touch of a child.

Good Morning, God

*Our Father which art in heaven, Hallowed be thy name.
. . . Thine is the kingdom, and the power, and the glory,
for ever. Amen.*   —*Matthew 6:9-13*

Once more my footsteps turn to the church of my childhood. I hear the organ and the voices in the choir. I sit in the stillness and worship. I listen to the scripture. I hear the minister speak the word of God. I hear him tell us to love one another as God loves. us.

I walk across the fields after church. A bluebird is singing in the fence row. The queen anne's lace nods in the breeze. A rabbit leaps through the fence. The air is warm and pure. A great blue heron silently sails across the blue sky.

God walks with me whether I am in the church or in the fields. God is everywhere. I am aware that the church has been the foundation of every great society. In every town in the United States, church steeples reach into the sky. I am mindful of the men and women in generations past who built this nation out of a wilderness. They left their graves along the overland trails. They left their names upon stained-glass windows. They built youth centers, hospitals, libraries, colleges, these people who believed in a better life and wanted to leave their children and grandchildren a finer world.

I say "Good morning" to you, God, because it is your spirit that has given man the desire to climb and to reach and to accomplish. Because of you, God, we have more than bread in our lives; we have roses too. Because of you we built civic theaters and little league baseball fields, preserved our national forests, wrote books of poetry.

I am writing the story of a glorious past in our lives. It is the foundation upon which to build the future. Our forefathers gave much to bring us what we have today. We too are working to usher in a world of freedom and opportunity.

Oh, Master, we can hear you calling, calling, "Come home, come home." We are coming, God. But along our way we are leaving a better rose, a better poem, a better hospital, a better chance for all to grow. Touch our lives, Master, touch our lives again and again that we may know that the glory of this earth is only a promise of what is to come. Take our hand and lead us into eternal life.

We know now, God, as we lift our eyes from the earth and the sun goes down and we rest, that thou art the kingdom, the power and the glory, forever.